Enough

Grace Edwards

BookLeaf Publishing

India | USA | UK

Enough © 2021 Grace Edwards

All rights reserved.

No part of this publication may be reproduced, stored in a retrieval system, or transmitted, in any form or by any means, electronic, mechanical, photocopying, recording or otherwise, without the prior written permission of the presenters.

Grace Edwards asserts the moral right to be identified as author of this work.

Presentation by *BookLeaf Publishing*

Web: www.bookleafpub.com

E-mail: info@bookleafpub.com

ISBN : 9789357447423

First edition 2021

DEDICATION

For Noah,

Who brought me Happiness

ACKNOWLEDGEMENT

First of all, I want to thank Bookleaf Publishing
for making my dream of becoming a writer
come true by making me a published author.
Noah Edwards, thank you for making me smile
everyday. Thank you for supporting me through
all we've been through together, and for
believing in me. I love you with all my heart!
Thank you Kylee Bustard for being my very best
friend since that fateful day in grade 6. You
pushed me to become a better writer and a better
person, and I could never have done this without
you. I'm so proud of you for making your
dreams come true too! I also want to thank
Allison Giggey, for always finding me books to
read, and for kindling my passion for writing.
Thank you, Lon Bechervaise. I can't express
how grateful I am for your wisdom and teaching
throughout the past few years. I've grown up to
be a capable women with a voice that I am not
afraid to use. Mom and Dad, thank you for
loving me no matter what. Tom Ryder, I love
you too. Gabe, keep being you.

PREFACE

This book of poems is about many different stories. Some of these poems are personal, but many of them aren't about me at all. They are about the people who I love and who mean the most to me. I've written about them to share their stories as best as I can, but they are only my perceptions. Everyone has their own story to tell.

Collapsing Galaxy

7 rotations around the sun.
Why aren't I like the stars?
Carefree,
Bright,
Blissful.
I'm weighted down
By my long hair.
Breathing
Already
Takes
Effort.
Don't share
Stay silent
No need to speak.

14 rotations around the sun.
My sun moved away,
Summer suddenly somber
Darkness
Closes in.
My search for a
New Sun
Ended in an old moon.
The moon became my
Best Friend

Because he watched me closely
When I couldn't sleep
He accompanied my
Lonely nights,
I stared at the stars
They silently watched me struggle
Suffer
Suffocate…
Choking on my tears I could only whisper
Through the sleeping walls
help.

15 rotations around a nonexistent sun.
No one noticed my
Pufferfish eyes
Dry, cracked smile,
Or my frantically duct taped heart.

16 rotations around a nonexistent sun.
Countless nights blurred my vision
I've never been so close to the

Edg
        e
Of the
World.
Terrified of the
Blank abyss
I lost my footing,

Grasping,
crazed,
to loose roots.

17 rotations around a nonexistent sun.
My tree
F
  E
    L
      L
Just two hands
Ten fingers
Holding me in this world
Finally I had the breathe to yell
"Help"
They finally asked me what's wrong.
"I'm falling,
I'm falling over the edge of the earth,
I'm not strong enough
To hold on,
Give me your hand."
They shake their heads,
Confused.
"Of course you can't be falling,
Baby,
The earth is round."

I broke
But I never let go

I couldn't take the weight
Of my hair
I slashed
It off
And braided myself a rope
I climbed
To solid ground
They were blind
I put my feet back on
My earth
THUMP
And I didn't stop
Raging
Roaring
Running
To the highest mountain,
To make sure I never
Come close
To the edge of the earth
Again.

I captured the sun
And superglued it into space
Chasing winter away
My smile brightened,
And stretched from one side of the earth to the
other.
I closed my eyes

And inhaled the fresh air
The stars winked down at me
You did it
They said
You finally fixed the Galaxy.

My Angel's Dust

Eons ago,
She dove selfishly into a dream,
Ecstasy,
Let me have a taste
She begged sweetly,
Just one.

Cigarettes stain her fingers
She takes a drag
exhales...yes
And alcohol poisons her flesh
She's stopped smelling baby's breath
Now she inhales white
Powder her nose
In the intoxicated room
Of angels
She loves passionately,
Bodily,
Baby,
Brokenly handing out pieces of her heart
Praying to god
That someone will stay,
She is the greatest star
Burning in the sky
Laughing while the brazen flames consume her

Until she is nothing but ashes,
Like the ones she used to drop
From her stale cigarettes.

Helpless Captivated

You will never understand
What it was like to watch you
fall in love.
The moment you met
Fate stepped in
Your love will be tragic
She whispered
As she covered your eyes in mist

My already too fragile heart
Couldn't survive another blow.
So I shut it off
built a bruised barrier,
Instead I chose to watch

As she toyed with your true love
Rejected your public advances
And Loved you in private,
I watched you shrink inside yourself
My eyes burned
I could not watch
You hurt so much

I drowned myself in oceans
Poured by the faceless

And found someone else to distract me
A wolf who
Gorged itself on women
Greedily hunted its prey
I didn't see its wake
One flash of its gold green eyes
I decided to fall
true love is a myth anyway

I don't know about you
But I split apart.
Smiling like I was happy
Being destroyed from the inside out,
Each word banged into my skull
Crack
Not enough
Worthless
You don't deserve him,
I was an
Imploding Star.

You have no idea
What it was like
To watch you fall in love.

Depression

Saturday
I miss a pill
An
Anti
Depressant
Because
I have
depression.
It stays
Away most
Days
But some days
It sneaks up on my
Like the monsters under my bed
Shadows hunting me for sport
Like the days I forget
My pill
And today
I hurt again.
Simple fights
And creeping doubts
Regrets
Haunting memories
Bring it back
In a torrent

I wish
I didn't need
antidepressants
to be happy.

Sins

My sin was at first a pond
That I only dipped
The tip of my toes in
Bravery didn't come easily to me
But she told me to come back
That's plenty
She thoroughly disciplined the rebellion out of
me
Or so she thought

Soon my sin became a lake,
Growing everyday
She said
Stop making mistakes
You're going the wrong way
This time though,
This time her discipline angered me
And my rebellion rushed

So when I found an ocean of sin
I dove right in
and now my skin is stained
but I forgive myself
And that is all I need

To be

13

Again

Collapsed on the hardwood floor
Drunk off my tears
Only the stars
Watch me break
Watch me burn
And the sun
Sees my hungover eyes
My rubbed raw nose
My chapped skin
early morning tiredness
my empty smiles
I see nothing worth keeping
And it starts
Again

Objectification in the 21st Century

He was staring
At my ass.
Your pants are tight
He said
Like that makes it okay
Despite yanking down my shirt
Too low
And hiking it up again
Too high
frustratingly
Hiding my straps

Make sure you're friendly,
But not too friendly,
Now you're being flirty
He's just a friend
He took you out,
Pay him what you owe,
Smile,
Not like that,
You look slutty,
That dress is so formal,

What's that problem with showing a little skin?
I said a little skin,
What are you preparing for
your "career as a stripper?"
I love girls who are natural
What's wrong with your face
Put some make up on

Make sure you look Good,
But not too good,
Or they'll say you were
asking for it.

Boys will be boys,
That's what they say,
Why are girls constantly appraised for their
appearance
Told to speak up,
And silenced once they dominate the
conversation,
You have such a beautiful smile,
Keep it closed.
Slimy eyes follow me around
Crawling me up and down

Smile
Do you have a boyfriend
Your number.
Every single time

I want to scream,
Fuck you
I'm a Person too

This is what a Dragon looks like:

A dragon is anger
With fire in its lungs
It doesn't like to be criticized
So it destroys
What undermines
This dragon is full
Of hate
Because she was neglected
So she makes people
Hurt like they
Hurt her
She is ferocious and fierce
Her claws kill
And she doesn't
Like to listen
To authority
So she burns bridges
And breaks the hearts
Of people who love her
Until she drives them away
And this dragon is left

Alone again
This dragon wasn't born
She was made.

Weightless

She walked on water
Light as air
The picture of grace
Not a care
In this world
She breathed
For herself
And when she opened her eyes
Everything changed
Because of who she saw
Standing before her
And when she tried to breathe again
Her chest was too heavy
And when she tried to take a step back
She began to sink
So when it grabbed her hand
And looked into her eyes
She held on
For her life
And this time when she breathed
She breathed for it
Because she didn't have the strength
For herself

Inadequate

Imperfection is inadequate
A message
I find
Everywhere.
Of course,
It's never said out loud
Because that would contradicting
Against everything we're told.
And yet
It follows me
When I stumble
And she hugs me tight
Too tight,
She says
You've got a good head on your shoulders
But you are wrong
Darkness
Will grab hold
Of your pure soul
Because heaven forbid
There be a little black mixed
into it's Snow White
I make mistakes
But I will not be forgiven for them
Because flaws,

Faults,
They destroy us
I'm sorry I'm not an angel
But I'm trying
My imperfections
Are more than adequate
To me

Perfection

One morning
I woke up from a dream
To the sleepy sound of your voice
Far over the phone
And my heart beat twice as fast
Because I was dreaming of
Perfection
And there you were
Bliss
But I was worried
Because dreamed
You asked me,
"Grace, do you love me?"
Do I love you?
How could I not love you!
I love your cute little
eye dimple
That hides behind your glasses
And your sense of adventure
Your sweet smile
that makes me smile too
No matter what
And your beautiful personality
So fucking full of happiness
Your ability to care

For me no matter what
Or why
Like 4 packs of halls
For my sore throat
And holding me when I am sick
and telling me I'm perfect
When we both know that's not true
That you will give me Everything
I want to give you Everything too

Snake

Right before the darkness
Takes over
I feel it's chill creeping through me
Slowly caressing my skin as it
Makes it's way to my-
End it
It whispers
As I travels up my veins
Too broken
It Echoes through my chambers
Destroy yourself
What's left of you
It slithers across my lungs
Squeezing like a starving python
Rivers pour out
Of my eyes
When it visits
The mirror multiplies it's shadows
I am helplessly
Heaving
Until I am too exhausted
To try breathing again

And when it finally crawls back into its hellhole
I wash my face

And pretend that I wasn't just
torn apart

The Wolf

Snarl
Harsh
Wild
Devastating
It is all consuming
Don't tempt it
It lacks self respect
Young girls beware
Innocent babies please listen
It will tear you apart
I promise

Not far from the tree
I
Could
N't
Stop myself
So I fell

It is from suicide and abuse
It is inebriated or otherwise
Out of its mind
Dangerous
Especially sober
It preys on insecurities

Takes advantage of intoxication
One after another
Trust me
You're not the first

It can speak
Whispering lovely lies
It cares for you
Seducing with each caress
You're heart may flutter
Maybe you will falter
Red
You better run.

It is cinnamon and smoke
Curling across the room
Inhale deeply
If you don't believe me
Baby girl
That's what it will
Name you
Own you
Fuck you
Over
And finally
Finish you off
And begin another
Hunt
For another

meal

Do what you will
Follow it's defined prints
Deep into the
Light intolerant
Lifestyle
Don't say I didn't warn you.

Lead Foot Annie

I didn't know her
But I wish I had
I just know
I would have loved
her smiling eyes
Her full-blown smile
The fact that
She didn't fear a thing
I would have sped down roads
Trying to catch up to her
She could have been a NASCAR driver
You know
I bet she gave the warmest
Happiest hugs
Sometimes I close my eyes
And listen for her laugh
The one that never stops
And makes you join in
I look at my hand
The gold she wore
And wish I could give it back
Hold her hand
Thank her for her loving son
He looks like her
His red hair shines like hers in the sun

And his foot is heavy too
His hugs are warm and happy
And I fell in love with him
I wish I could have had the chance
To meet the person who imparted so much
Genuine kindness,
laughter and slyness,
Especially stubbornness
I wish I could have
Had the chance
To love you like he does.

Our Sunrise

You drove while
We both sang
Until our overtired voices broke
But we kept singing anyway
Because love does that too you

The headlights beamed down on the yellow
brick road
We followed until this island's end
And every time I looked away
You looked at me
I could tell because of your huge smile
At 4am in the middle of
Nowhere

You were finally with me
So we watched each other
Watch the royal blue
Sunrise
Explode upon the day
We forgot about sleep
But you were as awake as the pink sky
And I think
In the moments before we left,
When you smiled at only me

I took my first step
To falling in love
With You

The Faithful

Their god
Determines their future
A voice in their head
Commanding in a whisper
Listen, he grumbles
She falls,
Weightless,
To her knees
Adamant
Save me please,
But pleas are useless
Everything is second to him
Her face is hard
Stone
Statues still crumble
She doesn't pray
Faithless,
But their faith is blinding,
Beautifully so,
They believe.
She breaks their hearts by needing them
As much as they need
Their god.

Aged

He is nine
And he is fifty-nine
Because he has lost too much
To be only nine
So he doesn't play games anymore
Because games are for kids
Who don't have craters in their hearts
And know what death looks like.

He is plagued by bad decisions,
Not his own,
Because nine year olds shouldn't have
To hunt for food,
And go to bed
Aching,
With the tv on
Because the night is too dark to sleep
Nine year olds have dads that
Play games
And take care of their boys
But remember
He is too old to play games
And his dad is too drunk
To feed him supper
Because drunk dads are assholes

And assholes only take
They don't give anything
But heartache
And this nine year old boy
Can't handle anymore of that
But he has to
And so he does
It makes him even older

He isn't nine anymore
But he is still too young
For all the hurt that has happened
He isn't fragile
Like you'd expect
He is stronger than the
diamonds his mom used to wear
Because he experienced a lifetime
When he was nine
He is present for every moment
And he knows exactly what he wants
Because life is too short
So he works so hard
And he laughs more than most
And tells you like it is
Not everyone likes his direction
Or that his is so real
But they are missing
Truth
Because he is full of truth

And he is Happy

37

Enough

Swirls of blank ink
Staining my sun bronzed skin
Remind me of my faults
My failures
Forgivenesses
But also
Of each new day
And every blessing I receive
Of the Love I have
The words tattooed on my body
Tell a story of where I am
How I learned
to love myself